CW00322060

Memoir of Sarah Knight

Knight

AN

MEMOIR

OF

SARAH KNIGHT,

WIFE OF THOMAS KNIGHT,

OF

COLCHESTER,

Who died on the 28th of the fifth month, 1828.

Philadelphia:

Printed and Published by

THOMAS KITE—64 WALNUT STREET.

—

1829.

PREFACE.

In the publication of the following Memoir, the friends of the deceased are influenced, solely, by the belief, that instruction and encouragement may be derived, by an extensive circle of her acquaintance, from the opportunity of tracing for themselves, in her own letters and memoranda, that gradual, but decided change of character, which was particularly apparent in the last three years of her life; affording an evidence, that the work of Divine grace in her heart, had, in good measure, subdued her naturally volatile temperament and unbending will; evincing, that in the trying hour of sickness, and in the awful prospect of death, she was favoured with that hope, which is "as an anchor of the soul, both sure and steadfast;" and whilst humbled under the consciousness of her own " pecu-

H T.

Samuel and
22nd of ninth
th of the fol-
ved by death,
eeks ; during
r dissolution,
er two dear
to know the
eighth month,
a second wife,
ting and im-
until she had
n years, after
rs at school.
ned under the
with Thomas
month, 1821.
found it diffi-
of her disposi-
ing principle
and she often
h her parents

liar unworthiness," was consoled with the evidence, that, through the mercy of the dear Redeemer, her sins were forgiven; and with the belief, that an entrance would be ministered unto her into His everlasting kingdom.

MEMOIR

OF

SARAH KNIGHT.

SARAH KNIGHT, daughter of Samuel and Mary Jesup, was born on the 22nd of ninth month,. 1798. In the fifth month of the following year her mother. was removed by death, after an illness of about two weeks; during which time, in the prospect of her dissolution, she expressed her belief, that her two dear children would not be permitted to know the want of a mother's care. In the eighth month, 1803, the surviving parent took a second wife, upon whom devolved the interesting and important charge of the daughter, until she had attained the age of about thirteen years, after which time she passed two years at school. On her return home, she continued under the parental roof, until her marriage with Thomas Knight, of Colchester, in the fifth month, 1821.

During her minority, Sarah found it difficult, from the extreme vivacity of her disposition, to cherish that self-denying principle which leads into true simplicity ; and she often keenly felt those restraints, which her parents

A 2

believed it their duty tenderly though firmly to
enforce, frequently evincing compunction on
account of the prevalence of her vain propen-
sities.

In reference to this subject, an extract from
a letter is here given, which she wrote in the
year 1818, to one of her young friends.

" If I had been but enough inclined to profit
by advice on important subjects, I see and believe, that ere this I should have missed many
an hour of remorse and sorrow." After other
observations, she adds : " My heart seems to
open unbidden, to pour forth its complaints to
one, who though far before me, can yet con-
descend to turn back, and cast an eye of pity
on those who, daily giving way to temptation,
and seeing their errors, sometimes *almost* ear-
nestly crave to be what their Creator intended
them to be—a people not conformed to this
world. Though we are not all called to the
same work, yet we may all forward the great
cause, by becoming preachers of righteousness
in conduct and conversation. This is what I
want ; but oh ! my very disposition is contrary
to every thing plain and simple."

After her marriage, there is reason to believe that her mind was renewedly visited by
Divine grace, and that she sincerely desired to
fulfil the duties of her new and important sta-
tion with propriety ; yet the extreme buoyancy
of her spirits, with good natural abilities, and
a peculiar quickness of perception, not unfre-

quently betrayed her into a too unguarded and
satyrical mode of expression, which, on reflec-
tion occasioned her to feel concern and deep
remorse.

In the spring of 1822, she became the mother of a little girl. She has often since been
heard to remark, that her love of taste was too
much suffered to prevail, instead of simplicity,
in her views respecting this interesting charge.

In the autumn of the same year she was visited with long and severe illness, which confined
her for several months; during which time
she was deeply humbled, under a consideration of former unwatchfulness, and was led to
desire, that greater circumspection might in
future prevail. Yet, when favoured with re-
turning health, the force of these impressions,
in degree, abated; she still stumbled at the
cross, and thus the growth of the pure seed
was retarded. But it pleased Infinite Mercy
to follow her with his chastisements, and in the
autumn of 1825 she had another long and severe attack of illness, when her recovery appeared doubtful. Under this dispensation, deep
instruction was sealed upon her mind; and
the truths of the Gospel were so mercifully
unfolded, that the foundation was laid for that
decided change of character, which was *gradually* developed during the remainder of her
life.

A memorandum, dated 5th of the eleventh
month, 1826, referring to this illness, was

found after her decease, which is here intro-
duced.

"And now, oh! how shall I commemorate
the Almighty's gracious and wonderful condescension to me, who has plucked my feet, in
degree, out of the mire and clay, and set them
upon a rock; and hath put a new song into
my mouth, even praises to our God! Humility
and gratitude, I think I endeavour to pray for.
It is now about twelve months since I lay ill
of a brain fever, and the mercy and goodness
I then experienced, may I *never* forget! I
think I then saw things too mighty for me to
record *now*. Oh! that I may not forget the
vows I then made; but rather, that I may
pray daily for strength to fulfil them in the
right time. Of late I have been much favoured with sensible goodness from on high. I
wish I may not feed too much upon it; but rather be willing to go down into the deep."

The following letters also refer to the same
period.

"I confess to thee that I have been troubled
with a reasoning mind; and it pleased Infinite Wisdom, in His adorable mercy, when I
was laid on that bed of sickness, which I hope
and pray I may never forget, clearly to unfold
some of the mysteries which my poor weak nature had at times stumbled at; and so clearly
to point out the *necessity* and efficacy of the
Saviour's *atoning sacrifice*, for otherwise lost,
fallen man, that I can never describe how

much my whole soul was wrapped in admiration and thanksgiving at the stupendous mercy. I was then instructed to see, that it was not for me to attempt to dive into the *why* and the *wherefore;* but that, without a Saviour or Redeemer, we had been lost for ever ; and whoever is favoured to gain an admittance into the heavenly city, it will be through the redeeming power and atoning sacrifice of our Lord and Saviour Jesus Christ. Wonder not, then, that redemption, through faith in the mediation and atonement of a crucified Saviour, should be a leading feature of my heart."

From the time of her recovery, she appears to have been engaged in desire daily to maintain the warfare, and to press forward towards the mark for the prize of her high calling of God in Christ Jesus ; and that she might be enabled to surrender her will and affections, to Him who had graciously visited her soul. She had for some years believed, that if she were faithful to manifested duty, it would be required of her publicly to espouse the Lord's cause ; and when the time drew near, for this open and avowed dedication, the recollection of her former unwatchfulness and inconsistencies often humbled her spirit ; and much fear pervaded her mind, lest she should move in such an awful work, before she had endured the necessary baptism for the refinement and purification of the vessel. The exercises and conflicts of her mind on this subject, are strik-

ingly conveyed, in letters to two or three inti-
mate friends, from which the following para-
graphs are extracted.

9th *mo.* 1826. "I wish to tell thee, I hope
in great simplicity, that I have long, perhaps I
might say for years, believed, that if I ever became what my Heavenly Father designed, I
must occupy some conspicuous part in the
church: this my nature has always shrunk
from, *more than I can describe.* Much, very
much dross remains yet to be taken away, before I can acceptably lift up a finger for the
Law and the Testimony. I often think, how
much more difficult it is to purify some vessels
than others."

10th *mo.* 1826. "Humility, faithfulness, and
obedience, are what I do desire to pray for.
Oh! there are times when it seems as if it
would be meat and drink to do the will of our
Heavenly Father ; and I would almost say, I
long for the right time to offer the sacrifice.
Then again I faint, and am ready to beg to be
excused ; and I believe I feel it harder than
many, to give up my own strong high will, and
to be redeemed from the many hindering things,
and, above all, the reasonings. The things I
most fear are disobedience, with all its attendant darkness ;—the construing the workings
of an active and nervously weakened imagination into a command, and so being almost
worse than disobedient ; and the fear of man !
But oh ! while I write, I feel as if nothing

could be so sweet as the firm belief that I should be enabled ' to do thy will, O God, and therein to experience preservation."

10th *mo.* 1826. " Simple obedience I have fervently prayed for ; and what a mercy, that he who knows the sincerity of the heart, will, in his own good time, make the way plain, and perhaps easier than my doubting heart sometimes allows me to view it. And yet, let me tell thee, that if any little sacrifice has been called for and yielded to, how precious, how great, how unspeakable, how abundantly transcendent to the gratification of our own will, has been the reward of peace ! I feel disposed to say, that if I am entrusted with the one talent, to occupy in any conspicuous way, I do believe the right time is not yet come : but oh ! may it be the ' ram caught in the thicket,' rather than I should *profess* more than I *possess.* I do believe, my endeared friend, that it is good, very good, to pray to lay aside all anxiety with respect to future steppings : I think I feel it from a *degree* of experience."

11th *mo.* 4. 1826. " It seems due to thee to tell thee, that I do believe thy words were blessed to my distressed heart ; and since thou left, I have enjoyed something of a calm hope and faith, to which I have for some days been a stranger. And it does appear to me, with clearness and comfort, that he who has in great mercy already forgiven so much, will not cast off his poor little child for a fearful holding back. Not but that I acknowledge to a feeling of great reasoning, and am, perhaps, too willing to make use of a cautious feeling as an excuse. For the cross is such, that it seems as if flesh and heart would fail under it ; and yet I can with truth say, I never did once ask to recant the covenants I have made in days of close trial."

The following letter was written a few days before her appearance in the ministry, dated in the 10th month, 1826.

"I have just been reading 'Thorpe's Letters,' beginning at page 29, which, I think, I have not read without some accession to my comfort. I do feel so great a desire to beg from thee a promise of remembrance and interest in thy best moments, that I do think I may safely tell thee so : I think I never needed them more. I was rather singularly attacked with illness last evening ; but a conflict *within* was beyond, far beyond it, for which I could not account, nor do I think it is well to try to do so. I was, however, favoured with a good night, and arose this morning with many anticipations of the privilege of assembling with some of my friends to-day. I hoped to get a little fresh strength ; but, alas, from this I am prevented ; and I am inclined to think, it is well that I have attended to what human prudence dictated. I find quiet, peaceful resignation more difficult to attain to, than perhaps at some former times ; yet I do trust that I am under Divine notice, and that it is in wisdom I may be deprived of instrumental aid. Could I describe to thee the peculiarity of my feelings, I might almost say *conflict*, thou wouldst, I know, sympathize with me."

On the 5th of the eleventh month, 1826, she first appeared in the ministry, in her own meeting at Colchester. The peace of mind which succeeded this public act of dedication is described in the following memorandum.

"Oh! what can I render to a very merciful Providence, for his goodness and condescension to such a worm as myself, amidst innumerable weaknesses and infirmities. On first day morning, the fifth of the eleventh month, it pleased Infinite Wisdom first to call upon me to open my mouth in a meeting of Friends in this town. I stood up with these words: 'A Saviour, or I die; a Redeemer, or I perish forever.' And oh! the flood of comfort I was permitted, in unmerited mercy, to feel poured into my poor mind! Oh! my soul, let me often recur to this time; and never let me forget the condescending goodness of a merciful Redeemer. The conflict and exercise I had undergone, produced some indisposition; but all feeling of bodily ailment was taken away, in the feeling of peace and happiness the heart enjoyed. Here too, I must record a remarkable visit I had from a very dear, valiant, and faithful servant, who visited me on the sixth-day before I appeared in meetings. As far as

B

any instrument was ever permitted to be useful
to me, this dear friend was. I have several
times, of late, believed myself called upon to
say a few words in meetings; and oh! how
shall I express the humble gratitude which
ought to pervade my heart, for the support graciously extended at such times. But how have
I to deplore the reasonings of the creature, so
that faith has not been in that exercise it ought
to have been. I trust, nevertheless, I can ap-
peal to Him who knoweth the heart, if I have
not fervently desired to be found in the simple
path of obedience; although, to a high stub-
born nature, like mine, I find it hard work."

The subjoined letters further pourtray her
feelings relative to her call to the ministry.

11th *mo.* 6. "With respect to my own
poor self, it is gratitude, humble, heartfelt gratitude, I desire to offer, and which I trust I do
feel a portion of. Pray that we may rejoice
with trembling. Whilst I am writing, I afresh
feel that it will only be by 'deaths oft,' that I
can hope to obtain preservation; so numerous
are my weaknesses and besetments. Oh! who
needs despair of the mercy of God through
Christ Jesus, whilst I can lift up my head in
hope. Let me tell thee, that after a conflict
which I connot, dare not describe, (and yet, I
am ready to think, not more severe than on
some former occasions,) how mercifully *clear
was the command,* and strength vouchsafed beyond finite conception. Oh! I can only say,

marvellous loving-kindness! abundant mercy! making previous conflicts and sufferings all light, and comparatively nothing. I think I cannot close without saying, 'Great and marvellous are thy works, Lord God Almighty; just and true are all thy ways, thou King of saints.' "

11th *mo.* Oh! if I could with sufficient gratitude acknowledge the transcendent excellency and ten-fold reward of endeavouring to perform the Divine will! Whilst I write, I feel myself as a brand plucked from the burning, permitted to testify that it is so; but I think I do desire to write cautiously. I often feel instructed in thinking of Peter's denial."

11th *mo.* 14. " I believe I may safely confess to thee, that of late the call from the Divine Master, to show myself openly on whose side I am, has been so loud and so searching, that I think I have at times sincerely desired, and fervently petitioned, that my will might be laid low. The conflict has very much affected my natural strength."

From this time, until indisposition prevented her attendance of meetings, she was frequently engaged, in a weighty and impressive manner, to espouse her great Master's cause; and there is ground to believe, that short as was her course of dedication, it will long be remembered by many who witnessed it.

The following extracts from her letters, evince an earnest desire to be preserved from going before her Guide in the exercise of her gift ; whilst she dreaded to be inattentive to the clear manifestations of the Divine will.

In the eleventh month, 1826, she writes to a friend :

" It has peculiarly, of late, appeared to me, that though we should by all means keep up a social intercourse, that we must 'come out and be separate,' and appear as fools ; for I do believe there are many things in our camp, tasted and handled, that the pure truth bears witness against. Wherefore this load that I feel ? It seems to me that offence is taken at the character of her who stands up to speak in the name of our great Creator ; and if so, who can marvel ? And yet, there have been as great wonders before, wrought by Him who has declared He can make even the greatest sinner, ' white as snow.', I cannot describe the fear I feel, that the *woe* is not enough felt ; but I also feel, if possible, a daily increase of the weight of the ' woe is unto me, if I preach not the Gospel.' He who knows the secret of the heart, only knows how fervently I at times desire to do right ; although, how do I have to lament a mixture of the old nature! Never, perhaps, had I more need to pray for humility and self-abasement. I think I have been able to pray, that the fire and the sword might destroy all that remains to be 'of the earth, earthy ;' and something whispers within me, much is yet to be done. Oh! all my soul prays, that there may be a patient abiding under the operation ; but I feel that I am often wresting myself from under the Holy Hand. Oh! to such a state am I brought, that I seem as if the bitterest draught of inward exercise, that I could believe was effecting the great work of the purification of my vessel, would be acceptable, could I believe, it was not from any unwatchfulness or disobedience on my part, but as a part of the necessary process of the fire and the sword."

1827. "Oh! the excellence and beauty of endeavouring to love and serve our gracious Lord, with all our heart and strength! But oh! the flattening, deadening fear, lest something of the activity of the creature should get in ; and this fear, surely, must be necessary for *me* to cherish. Notwithstanding the baptisms and conflicts necessarily attendant on a growth in the *root* of divine life, how transcendently more excellent this state, than that of the superficial Christian."

The subject of this memoir having, in adorable mercy, been made sensible, "that there is no joy to be compared with the joy of God's salvation," felt an earnest solicitude that her young friends might also be brought to the same blessed experience ; and she was frequently engaged, both in public and private, to convince them how inexpressibly sweet and precious is that peace which is vouchsafed to those who yield submission to the yoke of

Christ.   The fear she felt, lest, from the natural vivacity of her disposition, she should, in
her intercourse with her young friends, be-
come a stumbling-block in their way, is evi-
dent from the remarks contained in the following letters.

"I sometimes fear, that some of my friends
who are ready to hope good things for me, are
not aware of my *domestic* life and character,
and cast of feeling.   'Oh! it is in domestic life,
in the every-day qualities of the mind, that a
Christian character ought to shine.   Oh! pray
for me, look at the situation in which I am in
all respects placed, and tell me if it is not an
awful one, and enough to draw from me many
an anxious sigh.   I feel that I love the dear
young men that surround our table ; but when
a remark arises which I would fain express,
to assure them we are not unmindful of their
best interest, my own volatility presents itself
in array before me, and I feel convinced, that
precept without example is poor indeed. Yet,
when I have looked at the subject in the clos-
est manner, I think I have seen that religion
is recommended by an innocent cheerfulness,
rather than the reverse ; but it is the innocence
that is wanted."

"I desire to feel it a fearful thing to look to
human counsel ; but I want thee to pen me
down thy sentiments and advice on the subject,
the important subject, of conduct and conversation before my young friends, without *exact*

regard to minority of age. This is a subject, dear friend, which often calls forth the anxious sigh; because I am so fearful, on the one hand, of evincing a levity or impropriety of conduct, which would cause the way of truth to be evil spoken of; whilst on the other, I would yet more carefully avoid any thing like a 'stand by thyself,'* because that is contrary to every feeling of Christianity; and it should appear so to thy poor friend, more than to any one else, who is ready to acknowledge herself a spectacle of mercy, if she may but hope to be preserved amidst dangers on every hand, and which seem to increase. I have often observed, I have thought, to the injury of religion, the sackcloth worn too much outwardly; we are to anoint, and not to appear unto men to fast.''

"How truly humiliating it is, to find how much I am influenced by surrounding things. Oh! 'to lay aside every weight and every burden, and the sin that doth so easily beset us ;' —could I do it in *reality* and *sincerity.* Oh! when I see the ardour with which trifles are pursued, my very soul loathes them, and I seem as if I could pray for the enlightening of the dear young people, with all my heart and soul: not that I would infer that I am not often engaged with things that make me blush to recur to. Of late I have felt a dryness (although

* Isaiah, lxv. 5.

not unaccompanied with frequent breathings
and exercise of spirit) that discouraged me,
and causes a depression of lively faith and
hope, that grieves me. *Let me have an interest in thy most fervent prayers.* Shall I confess to thee, that many times when in the social circle, for years past, I have felt, indescri-
bably felt, the want there is amongst many, of
a more deep in-dwelling near the Fountain of
Good, which would greatly tend to the growth
of the Christian virtues, and not obstruct innocent cheerfulness."

"I need not say, remember thy poor weak
sister. I seem as if I should need thy remembrance, if possible, more than ever, on account
of the desires I feel, and my insufficiency to
fulfil these desires, not to disgrace the appearance I am conscious I in some measure make,
of the Christian character, before my youthful
relatives. Oh! pray, that though I can do
nothing to promote the cause, I may cast no
tarnish over the loveliness and brightness of
religion, in the view of their youthful minds.
Above all, pray for my increase in *humility*, in
deep *self-abasement*, under a more awful sense
of what unutterable Mercy has done for me,
and what yet remains to be done."

Her health, during the latter periods of her
life, was very delicate, and she had frequent at-
tacks of indisposition. These dispensations
afforded her much time for quiet retirement,
and were undoubtedly mercifully intended for

her instruction and refinement. The favoured
state of her mind, under these privations, may
be gathered from letters written during some
of these seasons of trial; extracts from two of
which are here given.

"Thou judgest rightly, that even bodily af-
flictions may be made subservient to our best
good. May I experience this: I think I may
say, with humble hope, that I have in degree
experienced it. Many times, when my kind
friends have expressed sympathy and concern
for my privations and illness, I have felt that I
did not need it—that I had comforts and re-
sources beyond every enjoyment that health
only can bestow. Oh! then, how can I evince
my gratitude to so condescendingly gracious a
God? surely only by simple obedience. I
have always found the enemy very busy at such
times, in endeavouring to occupy the mind in
too frivolous a manner; and yet I should be
truly ungrateful, if I did not acknowledge the
heavenly, peaceful, sometimes almost raptur-
ous seasons I have experienced; the consideration and acknowledgement of which, while I
am writing, humbles me into the depths of in-
significance. Mercy, unbounded mercy, I can
indeed sing of; not but that, indeed, when
taking a close scrutiny, I have to deplore time
misspent, favours unnoticed, and tempers un-
controlled. And yet, to be so favoured with
quiet, peaceful, soul-sustaining feelings! I of-

ten think, ' Oh! could the *worldling* know.' "
&c.

" Strong health I do not expect soon to be
in the enjoyment of, and I believe the want of
it to be, in the *permission* of a merciful Providence, for my good. I need often bringing
down: I find that my natural flow of spirits
betrays me into inconsistencies, alike hurtful
to myself and others. I am generally favoured to possess a calm peace, in a humble hope
of preservation; although, at times, ' the sea
and the waves roar;' and nature, that is to
say, unsubdued self, shrinks from the exclama-
tion of surprise, which a friend told me I need
not marvel at, ' Is Saul also among the pro-
phets!' In this view of things, the idea of
meeting many of my friends in the coming year,
often makes my heart ready to sink within me,
and the willingness to appear a fool was very
faint."

In the eighth month, 1827, the following
letter was sent by her to a friend. It will be
rightly appreciated, by those who have been
called to similar tests of faith and obedience
as are there pointed out.

" Perhaps thou mayst know from experience, what it is *not* to be able to express what
we feel, and what we would gladly give utter-
ance to. Such was, in some degree, my case
yesterday, during the few minutes we were
alone together, or I could have opened to thee
a heart, that feels indeed somewhat of that

which Paul describes, when he says, he had two spirits warring within him; and adds, 'Oh! wretched man that I am,' &c. Endeared friend, pray for me, that it may humble the creature to the very dust, to find how unwilling it is to yield up any trifle that is called for in the light of Truth. Well, in a little of that light which the great apostle had, when he wrote, 'Him that thinketh any thing to be unclean, to him it is unclean,' I think I saw, yesterday morning, that I must very much shorten my hair, and that too on that very day. I did so, just before you came; but couldst thou believe the conflict such a trifle occasioned, thou wouldst pity me, and I know thou wilt. But He who knows the heart, knows I did it in sincerity; and is, I apprehend, again showing me, that I must also make some alteration in my dress. This, too, is a close trial, and convinces me how unsubdued still is that nature which *at times* seems humbled into the dust, and which can rejoice in the hope of one day being 'set free from the law of sin and death.' Excuse my writing in such freedom: all do not understand these things, for experience only can teach them. I ought humbly and gratefully to acknowledge I had no reason to regret going to the monthly meeting. Thou wilt suppose I felt myself a spectacle indeed; for I had to testify that nothing but obedience to manifested duty will bring peace; and I also apprehended it essential to that *peace,* to put up the vocal petition."

Her last illness, which commenced in the 10th month, 1827, originated in taking a severe cold, which was followed by the rupture of a blood-vessel, an occurrence which had taken place once in a former illness. This was succeeded by an intermitting fever, which confined her to her bed for several weeks at a time, and which was never entirely subdued; though she was for some time so much relieved from the severity of the attack, as to admit of her being brought down stairs, to spend some hours daily in the family.

About the middle of the fourth month, 1828, a great increase of debility, with symptoms decidedly consumptive, were so apparent as to occasion the most serious apprehensions in the minds of her affectionate husband and near connexions. She was at times able to enjoy the company of her friends, till within a few days of her decease, to some of whom she gave affectionate counsel. She apppeared during her long affliction, to be gradually preparing for an eternal inheritance.

On the 26th of the fourth month she said: " It is one of my principal desires at this time, to endeavour after resignation to the Divine will as to the termination of my illness. I find human nature very weak. At times I am induced to query whether the wish to live does not centre in my dear husband and precious

child ; and yet, at others, I believe the thought
of having to magnify the name of my dear
Redeemer, more than ever I yet have done,
far surpasses any consideration of an earthly
tendency, if, haply, I might be enabled, in
some measure, to make up for my great re-
missness in time past.''

On the 19th of fifth month, she said to a re-
lation: " It must be through stupendous mercy, if ever I am permitted to enter into happiness." On the 26th she said: " I clearly
see I dare not trust in any thing short of the
unmerited mercy of redeeming love ; what a
favour to get to this ! How peaceful I feel.
Sometimes I am afraid I am *too* happy and
peaceful ; but I believe it is the enemy who
tells me so." Seeing her husband deeply af-
flicted, she said : " We have found many hard
things made easy. If I am taken, I have clearly seen that thou and the dear girl will be won-
derfully supported." After some other remarks, she added, " All I have to do is to trust
in the dear Son of God, who has forgiven me
much." Her breathing becoming more difficult, she said: " Pray for me, dear Thomas—
I know thou dost : pray for patience that I
may not murmur. I have been mercifully
dealt with ; I have had but little suffering, but
this is humiliating indeed ; yet I can proclaim,
all is in mercy. Through the unmerited mercy of the dear Redeemer, I feel sweet peace.
I hope it is not the enemy at work." In a few

C

minutes she added, "Oh! no, I feel it is not; but I am assured it is substantial peace I feel." In the evening she took a calm farewell of her little girl; but was much affected after she left the room.

On the 27th, her father, brother, and sister, arrived at Colchester, when she appeared to be so far gone, that some hesitation was felt about introducing either of them into the sick chamber; but on her brother's entering the room, and sitting quietly out of sight, she asked who was present; and on being informed, and that her father and sister were below, she wished them to come up stairs, and said: "This is what I wished; but feared it could not be managed."

To her brother she said: "May we strive so to live, and so to walk, that we may all meet again." To her sister: "I charge thee, and I charge you all, seriously—tell the dear girls (meaning her other sisters) I charge them not to follow my example: tell them not to look to others for example, but to Him who has forgiven me. I regret that I set you such an example; but, through the mercy of Jesus Christ our Saviour, I am forgiven. He has forgiven much. I must testify of his goodness —mercy, mercy, is all I have to testify of." She afterwards enquired particularly after her sister's health, and said: "Take care of the poor body; but, above all, take care of the immortal part." One present observed, in allusion to the dear invalid, "What a favour that the immortal part has been cared for." To which she replied: "Remember, I particularly wish to keep in view my peculiar unworthiness."

In the course of this day she expressed a desire, that all her dear young friends might be instructed by her situation. "Tell them," said she, "that since Christ has visited my soul, I have experienced more true happiness than at any former period of my life. I was made sensible, on this bed, three years ago, that Jesus Christ died for me, and for all, rich and poor." Afterwards she said to a friend in attendance: "Dost not thou think the lamp is about going out?" who, in reply, alluded to the favour of her having a supply of oil in the vessel, and that, through redeeming mercy, the lamp would burn with greater lustre and brightness in the kingdom of heaven. She answered, "It will, it will: it is all love and mercy." In the evening she was permitted to feel some relief from suffering occasioned by the affection of her breath, and distinctly said, "I can now say, not my will, but thine, O God, be done. Grant me, I pray Thee, one of the lowest seats in thy kingdom—one of the lowest;" adding, "O righteous Father, if this cup of suffering may not pass from me, except I drink it, not my will, but thine be done."

A few hours before the close, she again said; "Pray for me that my patience may hold out to the end." A dear friend present was engaged to offer the vocal petition, for an easy passage and a happy dismissal from her state of suffering, when dear Sarah clasped her hands and exclaimed, "Amen and amen, saith my poor soul."

About a quarter of an hour previous to her dissolution, she said to one present, "My dear friend, I feel *so happy* in the prospect of futurity! surely it cannot be wrong." Reply was made : " My dear, do not doubt." She answered, " I don't, I don't."

A few minutes before her departure she requested to be turned on her side, after which she lay perfectly still. The gradually increasing shortness of her breathing only indicated the near approach of death, which occurred on fourth day-morning, the 28th of fifth-month, 1828, between two and three o'clock, when her redeemed spirit was permitted, we doubt not, to enter into the joy of her Lord. Aged about twenty-nine years.

MISCELLANEOUS

EXTRACTS FROM LETTERS,

WRITTEN BY SARAH KNIGHT,

To some of her Friends.

———

"I have sometimes found encouragement from remembering, whatever may be our besetments, that we may observe, in tracing the history of Christians, in all ages of the world, they also had their trials, their doubts, and their fears ; and it has often been a strength to me, to remember what a dear friend once said to me, that 'in proportion as I became a member of the true church, I must expect, and assuredly should be called, to fill up the measure of suffering, as a part that our Divine Redeemer partook of for our sakes.' I think I may safely acknowledge, that I find seasons of continued favour are not, to my sanguine temperament, most calculated to promote deep

C 2

dgment and feelings most fully assent, whilst
quent aberrations of action make me ready
fear. I desire to remember how frequently
ou recommendest watchfulness unto prayer :
here, and here alone, is safety. Desire for
e, dear friend, that I may be careful in this
ery important respect. How difficult I some-
mes find this to be, when surrounded by those
hom, I apprehend, are little aware of what is
assing in this apparently thoughtless mind,
nd who may be apt, alas! too justly, to call
n question my sincerity as a professor, and my
consistency as to appearance and conduct.
And yet, amidst all, oh! do I not know what
it is to turn within, and feel that ' anchor to
the soul, both sure and stedfast ?' Let us never lose sight of the beautiful *simplicity there
is in the Truth.* I confess there are times
when it appears before me with unspeakable
clearness and beauty. Oh! that I could keep
close to it. To stand aloof from the world's
dread laugh, I am perfectly sure is attainable,
through best help; but I have made myself
hard work to attain to it."

may tell thee, I was
to enjoy the retireme
hink I then saw, th
is to prevent, by hi
ntly resorting to pray.

growth, although exquisitely delightful to experience, and making up for many a conflict."

"It seems a relief to tell thee some of the things that often occupy a mind ready to sink, at times, with what is passing within it; and yet I should be ungrateful indeed, were I not to acknowledge, that since the sublime truths and hopes of religion came before me with threefold force, they have afforded me comfort, satisfaction, and enjoyment, which all my pursuits, of whatever kind, have never granted, even for a moment. Do not, however, suppose that I call myself ' a new creature.' Oh! that I could believe, ' old things were passed away.' If, indeed, they may be passing away, what a mercy! what a favour! Let us be thankful, humble, watchful. Look towards me as a poor creature just plucked from the mire and clay, who once had a hope in the most awful of hours, but only and solely with the thief on the cross. Now there are times, when, through great mercy, I seem as if I could cling to a ' hope full of immortality.' "

———

"The last few days appear to have afforded little opportunity for that ' recollection,' as Fenelon terms it, so ' desirable for the Christian to experience and *wait* in.' Whilst I write, I am ready to question, however, whether I can in sincerity call myself a Christian : my best judgment and feelings most fully assent, whilst frequent aberrations of action make me ready to fear. I desire to remember how frequently thou recommendest watchfulness unto prayer : —here, and here alone, is safety. Desire for me, dear friend, that I may be careful in this very important respect. How difficult I sometimes find this to be, when surrounded by those whom, I apprehend, are little aware of what is passing in this apparently thoughtless mind, and who may be apt, alas! too justly, to call in question my sincerity as a professor, and my consistency as to appearance and conduct. And yet, amidst all, oh! do I not know what it is to turn within, and feel that 'anchor to the soul, both sure and stedfast?' Let us never lose sight of the beautiful *simplicity there is in the Truth*. I confess there are times when it appears before me with unspeakable clearness and beauty. Oh! that I could keep close to it. To stand aloof from the world's dread laugh, I am perfectly sure is attainable, through best help ; but I have made myself hard work to attain to it."

———

" I may tell thee, I was favoured in some degree to enjoy the retirement of this morning ; and I think I then saw, that the work of the enemy is to prevent, by his insinuations, my frequently resorting to prayer, as being pre-

sumptive in me. But have we not the greatest encouragement to approach the footstool
of Divine mercy. Yet how often do I remember, ' if I regard iniquity in my heart, the Lord
will not hear me.' "

" Let us remember, that to devote every talent and faculty to the service of a crucified
Saviour, comprehends a great deal. Oh!
whilst I write, I feel how fearfully thy poor
weak friend falls short. Have we not with
sincerity supplicated at the footstool of Divine
Grace, to be enabled to devote every talent
and faculty to our Heavenly Father. Let us
then trust, that as we are daily engaged to offer our petitions, we shall be enabled to see
what is in the mixture, and to come out there-
from. I have of late been afresh convinced of
the necessity of our coming out from the hindering things, as much and as often as possible,
and endeavouring by prayer, to cast all crowns
at the feet of the Divine Master. Methinks
my dear friend will respond to the sigh, I can
but heave when I note this feeling, as I do my
own extreme unwillingness to give up all that
would gratify self, particularly in my pursuits
and habits, conduct and conversation.————
This afternoon, when we settled into silence,
and it seemed as if there were a little true abi-
lity, although in much weakness, to cast our-

selves at the footstool of Divine Mercy, clothed as we felt ourselves with infirmities, oh! how convincing was the feeling of the *transcendent excellency* of such holy quiet, of such heavenly calmness as we then felt: surely it warmed our hearts in a manner nothing earthly could? Yes, and it afresh convinced us, none of the things of time can satisfy the longings of an immortal mind."

"Let us endeavour to take no undue thought for the morrow; but let us pray to be preserved in calm dependence upon Him, who alone can preserve us. Think of thy poor friend, when surrounded by her friends of *various descriptions.* Oh! to bring no disgrace on the Truth, and to act with courtesy and kindness, without any compromise of best feeling and principle, seems too much almost to hope; but ah! what a mercy, we may pray for it!"

"I have of late more particularly had to remember, that it is only as we are brought into a conformity to the death of Christ, that we can expect to partake of His consolations; and I believe it will be often the lot of the *conspicuous* traveller Zion-ward, to be plunged

into the deeps : but then, that enduring of the
cross, and despising the shame.   Oh! we may
read of the peace resulting from it, in the experience of many Christians of all denomina-
tions.   What encouragement to look at what
others have passed through, and then to remember the declaration, ' My strength is made
perfect in weakness.' "

———

It will be seen by the dates of the two following letters, that they were written during
her last illness.   The last of them was in pen-
cil, when unable to use the pen.

11th *mo.* 1827. " Once again, yes, once
again, through the mercy of an adorable Providence, I thus commune with thee, with feelings of no common kind.   Oh! that they were
grateful enough, and humble enough.   Help
me, dear friend, to praise Him, who hath dealt
with one of the most unworthy of his crea-
tures, in so gracious and merciful a manner
that I cannot describe.   My heart trembles,
lest ingratitude should be my return ; and yet,
how oft do I lift up my heart to our all-pro-
tecting Saviour, that refinement may be ac-
complished.   Till now, I have not had strength
to write to thee, and this is an effort which
nothing but sincere friendship would induce
me to make.   I long to see dear ×——; do
hand her my dear love ; tell her not to pray

that I may be spared suffering ; but rather that I may be purified, by whatever means Infinite Wisdom may see best for one so frail."

1828. "I have indeed been mercifully dealt with, and sometimes I am, or apprehend myself, so condescended to, that I fear to believe the voice, lest it should originate in my own imagination, the workings of which I have an indescribable fear of; but a merciful Father knows how I lift up my heart to be preserved from this. It is amongst my fears, and doubts, and trials, lest, having so much leisure, it should not be improved. I am apt rather to look with anxiety at the future, instead of settling down at the present time, to the root of Divine Life, where is all power to raise me up again, if it be His holy will. I confess I feel strong ties to earth—my precious Thomas— my dear child ; and sometimes I think I have wished to live, if I might show myself a monument of redeeming mercy to other young people, to the glory of so gracious a Saviour."

THE END.

CPSIA information can be obtained
at www.ICGtesting.com
Printed in the USA
BVOW06*1154270317
479540BV00007B/46/P